Because

I HAVE FOUND IN JESUS CHRIST THE
ANSWER TO MY EVERY NEED, AND BECAUSE
I AM EAGER TO SHARE THE BLESSINGS OF
MY FAITH WITH OTHERS

I am happy to present this book to

_____

with the prayer

THAT THE READING OF ITS PAGES WILL LEAD
TO A DEEPER UNDERSTANDING OF THE GLORIES
OF THE CHRISTIAN FAITH AND TO A FIRMER
CONFIDENCE IN JESUS CHRIST, OUR SAVIOR

_____

SIGNED

What JESUS *Means to Me*

What
JESUS
Means to Me

◇◇◇◇◇◇◇◇◇◇◇◇◇◇◇◇◇◇◇◇

By H. W. GOCKEL

ESV Edition

CONCORDIA PUBLISHING HOUSE • SAINT LOUIS

This edition © 2008 by Concordia Publishing House
3558 S. Jefferson Ave., St. Louis, MO 63118-3968
1-800-325-3040 · www.cph.org

First edition © 1948 Concordia Publishing House
Hardback version: 06-1327, ISBN 13: 978-0-7586-1685-2
Paperback version: 06-1328, ISBN 13: 978-0-7586-1686-9

1 2 3 4 5 6 7 8 9 10   17 16 15 14 13 12 11 10 09 08

Contents

Preface

JESUS means more than the world to me. The last name to occupy my conscious thoughts at night—the first name to enter my waking mind each morning—is "the name that is above every name," the eternal name of Jesus.

But why?—What is it about the name of Jesus that bridges every day and night, that bridges every night and day, and goes with me wherever I might be? What is it in the name of Jesus that makes it the golden sunset of every evening, the bright and cheering dawn of every morning? Am I perhaps the victim of some sweet delusion?

By no means! Jesus is a fact. He is a tremendous fact. He is an eternal ever-present fact. He is the one sure fact around which everything in heaven and earth revolves. He was a fact "in the beginning," before the heavens and the earth were made.

And He is still the world's most powerful fact today—always present in the lives of those who believe in Him, always helping, always guiding; for He has promised, "Behold, I am with you always, to the end of the age."

Jesus is many things to me. He is pardon, peace, joy, hope, assurance, contentment, and life everlasting. He is my Friend, my Companion, my Counselor, my Prophet, my Priest, and my King. And He can be all of that for *you*. Indeed, He *wants* to be all of that for you. "Behold, I stand at the door and knock," He says. "If anyone hears My voice and opens the door, I will come in to him and eat with him, and he with Me."

The experiences and convictions that are recorded in this little volume are by no means to be regarded as the experiences and convictions only of the author. They are the glorious convictions of millions of Christian men and women throughout the world today: men and women in your town, in your neighborhood, perhaps on your own street.

They were the convictions of millions upon millions who lived and died during the long ages past. They were the deep and abiding convictions, for instance, of Horatius Bonar, who lived more than one hundred years ago and who summed up all his religious experience in the well-known lines:

> *I heard the voice of Jesus say,*
> *"Come unto Me and rest;*
> *Lay down, thou weary one,*
> *lay down Thy head upon My breast."*
> *I came to Jesus as I was,*
> *So weary, worn, and sad;*
> *I found in Him a resting place,*
> *And He has made me glad.*

Jesus can make *you* glad! What He has meant to hundreds of millions down through the centuries, and what He still means to uncounted multitudes today, He can mean to *you*. In order that you, too, might find in Him a "resting place," this book, by the providence of God, has come into your hands. If you have not learned to know Jesus Christ as the Son of God—your Savior, your Master, and your Friend—nothing is more important for you right now than that you read these pages. H. W. G.

Life

"For to me to live is Christ."

If you were to ask me what Jesus means to me, I could think of no better reply than these seven short words of the apostle Paul, written two thousand years ago.

The artist who spends the late and early hours in the company of his paint and brush and canvas may very well say, "For me to live is _art_." The musician who thinks and dreams and speaks of nothing but his music may very well say, "For me to live is _music_." In a similar but in an unspeakably higher sense, I can truly say, "For to me to live is _Christ_"!

In Christ I have found the final answer to my greatest needs, the abiding satisfaction of my deepest longings, the complete dispelling of my darkest fears, and the rich fulfillment of my

1

highest aspirations. Is it any wonder that I say, "For to me to live is *Christ*"?

There is not a blessing in my life that, if I trace it back to the hand that gave it, does not lead me back to the Son of God. No matter where I turn, no matter where I look—if there is anything good, anything true, anything that has brought lasting joy and gladness into my life—I recognize it ultimately as a gift that has come to me through faith in Jesus Christ, my Savior.

In Him, above all, I have found complete forgiveness for all my sins. The Bible tells me that He "loved me and gave Himself for me." It assures me, "The blood of Jesus His Son cleanses us from all sin." And it promises, without qualification, "Whoever believes in Him should not perish but have eternal life." Because I believe these promises and have been assured by God Himself that they are true, I can spend every hour of the day in the full assurance that I am prepared to meet my God. My sins have been forgiven through faith in Jesus Christ, my Lord.

This knowledge has filled my heart with a peace and joy and hope that mere human words can never utter. The poet despaired of ever finding words to describe the thrill of a life that had found its peace with God through faith in Christ, when he penned the words:

> *The love of Jesus, what it is,*
> *None but His loved ones know.*

I have that peace. I am assured of that love. Through Christ I have been born into a life of assurance and joy and hope. Through Christ I have been made a child of God and an heir of heaven.

That is why I can say with the apostle Paul and with all Christians of all ages: "Christ is my life."

> *As the branch is to the vine,*
> *I am His, and He is mine.*

I am bound to Him by a debt of gratitude that all eternity could not pay. And He is bound to me by a love so limitless that no measurement could ever plumb its depths.

It is this close and intimate relationship with Jesus Christ, the Son of God, that is the source of my inner strength and joy. In this close relationship with Him, I have found the only answer to the deepest cravings of my soul: pardon, peace, power, provision, companionship, hope, truth, assurance, joy, and heaven.

And having found these, I have found *life*—life, full and free; life, glorious and triumphant; the "abundant life," which God has guaranteed to those who come to Him through Jesus Christ, His Son. I have experienced what millions of other believers have learned, namely, that "if anyone is in Christ, he is a new creation. The old has passed away; behold, the new has come."

Among the old things that have passed out of my life are sin and guilt and fear; uncertainty and doubt and dark despair. And among the new things that have entered my life are assurance of God's love, assurance of His guidance and protection, companionship with Christ, and the certain prospect of eternal life with Him in heaven. "The old has passed away," indeed; "the new has come."

These are the glories of the Christian life, the life that is "hidden with Christ in God." And these are the glories that we shall take up, one by one, in each of the succeeding chapters of this book.

Only he who can say with the apostle Paul, "For to me to live is Christ," can complete the sentence as Paul first spoke it—"and to die is gain."

> *O Jesus, King most wonderful!*
> *O Conqueror renowned!*
> *O Source of peace ineffable,*
> *In whom all joys are found:*
>
> *O Jesus, light of all below,*
> *The fount of life and fire,*
> *Surpassing all the joys we know,*
> *All that we can desire:*
>
> *May ev'ry heart confess Your name,*
> *Forever You adore,*
> *And, seeking You, itself inflame*
> *To seek You more and more!*

Pardon

Of all the things that Jesus means to me, He is, above all else, my Savior. By His suffering and death *in my place* upon the cross He has paid the penalty of all my sins. The Bible assures me that though my "sins are like scarlet, they shall be as white as snow; though they are red like crimson, they shall become like wool." And why? Because "the blood of Jesus His Son cleanses us from all sin."

I know that to many people today the word *sin* does not mean very much. Sin, they say, is a mistake or a fault that can't be helped and which therefore is not so serious. Sin to many people is just a flaw that somehow or other will be forgotten when God begins to settle His accounts. There are men and women who shrug off the idea of sin as being "just one of those things."

7

But God thinks otherwise. No matter how lightly men may speak of sin, no matter how cleverly they may seek to explain it or excuse it, God has placed His curse upon it. "The soul who sins shall die." "The wages of sin is death." "Cursed be everyone who does not abide by all things written in the Book of the Law, and do them."

Sin, according to God, is a frightful thing that, if it remains unforgiven, will result in the eternal separation of a man from his Maker.

I know, too, that some people associate the idea of sin only with criminals: with murderers, adulterers, and public scoundrels. But God says, "There is no distinction: for all have sinned." "They have all turned aside; together they have become corrupt; there is none who does good, not even one." "There is not a righteous man on earth who does good and never sins." "We have all become like one who is unclean, and all our righteous deeds are like a polluted garment." "Whoever keeps the whole law but fails in one point has become accountable for all of it."

Those are God's words.

In His sight there is no difference, as far as the fact of sin is concerned, between the celebrity socialite, the respectable family man, the loving mother, the refined librarian, and the man who was sentenced last week to die for murder. There may be a difference in degree. But there is no difference in the fact. For "the Scripture imprisoned everything under sin." "There is no distinction."

According to God's reckoning, sin is every departure from His holy will in thoughts or words or deeds. To have an impure thought, to say an unkind word, to be disrespectful, envious, or quarrelsome, is just as surely a sin as are robbery, theft, or wicked violence. Jesus told the people of His day that hatred and anger were an infraction of God's commandment: "You shall not murder." If that is true, and Jesus says it is, then who can count the sins of which every one of us is guilty every day of his life?

There are people to whom this consciousness of sin has never become very real. While they

are ready, in a general way, to admit their
shortcomings and regret them, they have
never been crushed or terrified by the dreadful
implications of their sin. The great apostle Paul,
when he became conscious of the terrific burden
of his guilt, cried out: "Wretched man that I am!
Who will deliver me from this body of death?"
The piercing pain of sin had cut deep into his
anguished soul.

David, the man after God's own heart, when
he came to realize that his sins were great enough
to separate him from the presence of God into
all eternity, exclaimed: "When I kept silent, my
bones wasted away through my groaning all day
long. For day and night Your hand was heavy
upon me; my strength was dried up as by the
heat of summer." David had learned the terrible
reality of his sin and the still more frightful
reality of sin's consequences. Sin, *his* sin, had
become real to him—frightfully real!

I, too, have felt the dreadful weight of sin.
Again and again I have had to say with the
apostle Paul: "I know that nothing good dwells

in me, that is, in my flesh." With David I have had to confess: "Behold, I was brought forth in iniquity, and in sin did my mother conceive me." As I look back to my childhood days, I see the undeniable truth of God's verdict: "The intention of man's heart is evil from his youth." I must agree with Him when He says that by nature I was among "children of wrath, like the rest of mankind."

But why speak about my sin—when I began to speak about my Savior? Because no man can tell what Jesus means to him until he has first told what *sin* has meant to him. To tell the full story of a rescue at sea, one must first tell the story of the shipwreck that made that rescue necessary. No man is ready to accept Christ as his Savior from hell and damnation until he has felt the hot breath of hell blow over his quivering conscience. If Christ is to be our Savior, we must know from what we must be saved.

Right here is where Jesus stepped into my life and filled it with a joy and a peace which surpass all understanding. For in Him I have God's assurance of full and free forgiveness of the entire burden of my sin. Without Christ there would have been, there could have been, no forgiveness. Without Christ the course of my life would have led straight to a judgment that would have been too terrible to contemplate. For "no man can ransom another, or give to God the price of his life, for the ransom of their life is costly and can never suffice." "There is salvation in no one else, for there is no other name under heaven given among men by which we must be saved." No other name than the blessed name of Jesus!

The Bible tells us, "When the fullness of time had come, God sent forth His Son, born of woman, born under the law, to redeem those who were under the law, so that we might receive adoption as sons." Christ, the eternal Son of God, came down from heaven to accomplish what I was unable to do—and He did it in my place, as my substitute.

I was unable to keep God's Law. So Christ

kept it for me. The commandments that I have
broken *He has kept*—and His record has been
written to my account. That is the wonderful
assurance that God has given me in the fourth
and fifth chapters of Paul's Epistle to the
Romans. What I could not do, Christ did for
me. And now, to use the word of Scripture,
God has "imputed" Christ's righteousness to
my account. He has written *His* record to *my*
credit! Paul says: "Not having a righteousness of
my own . . . but that which comes . . . from God
that depends on faith."

> *Jesus, Thy blood and righteousness*
> *My beauty are, my glorious dress;*
> *Midst flaming worlds, in these arrayed,*
> *With joy shall I lift up my head.*

But more! Christ also suffered the
punishment of all my sins. He assumed the
guilt that was mine. He paid the penalty that
I should have paid. He took my place before
the bar of God's justice and by His payment
of my debt secured my freedom. Because of

Christ's atonement I have been acquitted. This atonement theme is the golden thread of assurance that God has woven throughout the pages of the Bible.

Already seven hundred years before Jesus was born, the prophet Isaiah looked forward to the Savior's death on Calvary and wrote, "Surely He has borne our griefs and carried our sorrows. . . . He was wounded for our transgressions; He was crushed for our iniquities; upon Him was the chastisement that brought us peace, and with His stripes we are healed. All we like sheep have gone astray; we have turned—every one—to his own way; and the LORD has laid on Him the iniquity of us all."

Jesus Himself, speaking of the purpose of His coming into the world, said that He had come "to give His life as a ransom for many." In the night in which He was betrayed, He gave each of His disciples a piece of bread with the words, "This is My body which is for you." And He gave them the cup with the words, "This is My blood of the covenant, which is poured out for many for the forgiveness of sins." His death in the place of sinners was to purchase forgiveness for all mankind.

Late one night, speaking to a leader of the Jews, Jesus revealed the purpose of His coming into the world and particularly the purpose of His suffering and death. He said to Nicodemus, "As Moses lifted up the serpent in the wilderness, so must the Son of Man be lifted up, that whoever believes in Him may have eternal life. For God so loved the world, that He gave His only Son, that whoever believes in Him should not perish but have eternal life."

This was the glorious fact that the apostles proclaimed throughout the world soon after Christ's ascension into heaven. "Christ died for our sins." "We were reconciled to God by the death of His Son." "The blood of Jesus His Son cleanses us from all sin." "He Himself bore our sins in His body on the tree [the cross]." "[He] loved me and gave Himself for me." "Christ redeemed us from the curse of the law by becoming a curse for us." "You were ransomed

...with the precious blood of Christ." "If anyone does sin, we have an advocate with the Father, Jesus Christ the righteous. He is the propitiation [the reconciliation] for our sins, and not for ours only but also for the sins of the whole world." These are all direct quotations from the Bible, written by men who had been commissioned by Christ to spread His saving Gospel.

In view of these clear Bible statements, what does Jesus mean to me? Above all else, He means forgiveness! His life, His suffering, His death were all for me. Through faith in Him, I have come to share in the unspeakable assurance of those of whom the apostle says, "There is therefore now no condemnation for those who are in Christ Jesus." No guilt! No fear! No condemnation! For all my sins have been washed away in the atoning blood of Christ.

It was after the apostle Paul had contemplated the marvelous love of God in Christ that he burst forth with the jubilant hymn of faith, "What then shall we say to these things? If God is for us, who can be against us? He who did not spare His own Son but gave Him up for us all, how will He not also with Him graciously give us all things? Who shall bring any charge against God's elect? It is God who justifies. Who is to condemn? Christ Jesus is the one who died—more than that, who was raised—who is at the right hand of God, who indeed is interceding for us. Who shall separate us from the love of Christ? Shall tribulation, or distress, or persecution, or famine, or nakedness, or danger, or sword? . . . No, in all these things we are more than conquerors through Him who loved us. For I am sure that neither death nor life, nor angels nor rulers, nor things present nor things to come, nor powers, nor height nor depth, nor anything else in all creation, will be able to separate us from the love of God in Christ Jesus our Lord."

That is the supreme assurance of every man who comes to God through Christ. And that is *my* assurance. Through Christ, I have a loving God in heaven. Through Christ, the wall of partition between His Father and me has been broken down forever. Through Christ, I have free access to the Father-heart of God—because through Christ my sins are all forgiven. That is why I can join with the millions who confess:

> *Not what these hands have done*
> *Can save this guilty soul;*
> *Not what this toiling flesh has borne*
> *Can make my spirit whole.*

> *Not what I feel or do*
> *Can give me peace with God;*
> *Not all my prayers and sighs and tears*
> *Can bear my awful load.*

> *Thy work alone, O Christ,*
> *Can ease this weight of sin;*
> *Thy blood alone, O Lamb of God,*
> *Can give me peace within.*

> *Thy love to me, O God,*
> *Not mine, O Lord, to Thee,*
> *Can rid me of this dark unrest*
> *And set my spirit free.*

Thy grace alone, O God,
  To me can pardon speak;
Thy pow'r alone, O Son of God,
Can this sore bondage break.

I bless the Christ of God,
  I rest on love divine,
And with unfalt'ring lip and heart
  I call this Savior mine.

What does Jesus mean to me? He means many things. But, above all else, He means— *pardon!*

Peace

Two artists vied with each other to see which could produce a painting that would depict the idea of peace. One painted the picture of a quiet lake away up on a mountaintop. Not a breeze was stirring. Not a bird was flying. Not a ripple disturbed the quiet waters. All was perfect silence. That, in the opinion of the first artist, was the truest picture of peace.

The second artist painted a picture of a roaring waterfall, with a mighty tree hanging over it. In the crotch of a limb bending over the turbulent waters and almost within reach of the rising spray—he painted a tiny sparrow sitting calm and unperturbed upon her little nest. In the midst of the mighty roar, surrounded by what seemed to be frightful danger, the sparrow hadn't a worry in the world: her cozy little nest was snug in the crotch of a mighty oak—on a branch that the waters could not reach.

Both artists agreed that the second picture came closer to depicting the highest conception of peace. Perhaps neither of them knew that in the second picture they had found an excellent portrayal of the peace that a Christian believer has found in his Savior.

The true peace and rest of the Christian life is not a peace and rest that is to be found somewhere in a distant world of make-believe, but a peace and rest that is to be found right here in the very midst of a world of trial and trouble.

It was the night before His enemies nailed Him to a cross that Jesus said to His disciples— and to His followers of all time—"Peace I leave with you; My peace I give to you. Not as the world gives do I give to you. Let not your hearts be troubled, neither let them be afraid." "I have said these things to you, that in Me you may have peace. In the world you will have tribulation. But take heart; I have overcome the world."

In the world—tribulation; in Christ—peace. This is the experience of every believer, as it has been the experience of the children of God in all ages. There need be no denying the fact: this world is not a congenial place for the practice of the Christian life. I am not speaking of the world of joy and beauty that God has given us— the verdant meadows, the enchanting hillsides, the majestic mountain peaks, the blue canopy of heaven, and the soft and downy clouds that float like angel pillows across a summer's sky. No, all of this is lovely beyond description.

But I am thinking of the world in the sense in which the Bible often speaks of it—the human family as it exists apart from God. It is of that world that the Bible says, "Do not love the world or the things in the world . . . the desires of the flesh and the desires of the eyes and pride in possessions." That is the world of ugliness, of sordidness, of meanness, with which we find ourselves surrounded day in and day out—the world whose path is strewn with broken hearts and blasted lives and whose graves are watered with the tears of deep and dark despair.

In our passage through *that* world, says Jesus, we shall have tribulation. But—"in Me . . . peace"! That has been my great discovery. In Christ I have found peace in the midst of all adversity, peace in the midst of conflict, peace in the face of opposition, peace beneath the weight of every burden. The apostle Paul, toward the end of a life that had been beset by unnumbered difficulties, wrote to his friends, "[Christ] is our peace." What did he mean?

Above all, he meant that in Christ he had found peace with God. Paul had been a great sinner. He had persecuted the Church of Christ. But by the grace of God he had come to a shocking realization of his enormous guilt. "Wretched man that I am!" he exclaimed. He became conscious of a "dividing wall of hostility" that, if it would not be removed, would forever separate him from the presence of his God.

But—and this was the greatest revelation of his life—that wall had been removed! In spite of his sins, he and his heavenly Father were

on good terms. Christ had brought about a
complete reconciliation. That is why Paul could
write to the Romans, "Therefore, since we have
been justified by faith, we have peace with God
through our Lord Jesus Christ." That is why he
could end his letter to them with the familiar
greeting, "May the God of hope fill you with
all joy and peace in believing." And that is why
he could speak the familiar benediction upon
his fellow Christians, "The peace of God, which
surpasses all understanding, will guard your
hearts and your minds in Christ Jesus."

That peace of God is mine, and it is mine
through Christ Jesus. It is rooted forever in
the knowledge that, through Christ, God and
I are completely reconciled. We are "at one"
through the at-one-ment of the Savior. Let
my conscience accuse me, let the world point
its mocking finger at the record of my failures,
let Satan and hell seek to throw fear into my
soul by reminding me of the depths of my
iniquity—I say, let the devil, the world, and my
flesh try to rob me of the inner peace that I have

found in Christ's forgiveness—they shall never
undermine my heart's assurance:

> *Now I have found the firm foundation*
> *Which holds mine anchor ever sure;*
> *'Twas laid before the world's creation*
> *In Christ my Savior's wounds secure;*
> *Foundation which unmoved shall stay*
> *When heav'n and earth will pass away.*

> *Though earthly trials should oppress me*
> *And cares from day to day increase;*
> *Though earth's vain things should sore*
> *distress me*
> *And rob me of my Savior's peace;*
> *Though I be brought down to the dust,*
> *Still in His mercy I will trust.*

> *Let mercy cause me to be willing*
> *To bear my lot and not to fret.*
> *While He my restless heart is stilling,*
> *May I His mercy not forget!*
> *Come weal, come woe, my heart to test,*
> *His mercy is my only rest.*

That is the foundation, the cornerstone, on which my inner quiet rests. I am at *peace with God*. And being at peace with God, I am at peace with myself. I have received an inner strength that prepares me for all of life's challenges.

I am at peace in the midst of conflict. What if things are going wrong? What if, because of my loyalty to Christ, the winds of opposition blow stiff and strong? What if the waters of life are ruffled by the fierce storms of hatred and persecution? Let the storms rage. I am at peace with God! We are told that—no matter how furious the storm on the surface of the ocean, no matter how high the billows roll and how deep the watery valleys that stand between them— the deepest caverns of the ocean know nothing about the storms that rage above. Down there in the ocean depths all is calm, all is quiet. So, too, is the heart that has found its peace with God through Christ. No storm can disturb its inner quiet.

And I am at peace beneath the weight of every burden. It would be foolish and untrue to

say that the Christian life does not have its trials.
The gnawing pang of loneliness, the heavy hand
of sickness, the bitter pain of disappointment,
the icy finger of inevitable death—all of these
befall the Christian as they do every man. But
there is a difference, a great difference! Through
Christ, the believer knows he is at peace with
God and, being at peace with his Maker, he
knows that even sorrow and sickness and death
are part of God's *gracious* plan for him. And so
he rests in quiet peace beneath the weight of
every burden.

Above all, I shall dwell in peace when I
am called upon to make that fateful journey
through the valley of death. With Simeon of
old, I shall be able to welcome "Death's bright
angel" with the hymn of triumph, "Lord, now
You are letting Your servant depart in peace,
according to Your word; for my eyes have seen
Your salvation." With the sweet singer of Israel,
I shall be able to say, "Even though I walk
through the valley of the shadow of death, I will
fear no evil, for You are with me." And from

where shall I draw this courage? From the love of Christ, through whose life and death I am at peace with God.

The Bible tells us, "You keep him in perfect peace whose mind is stayed on You." Millions of believers will testify that they have found more positive psychology in those few words than in a whole library of technical volumes on the subject. Millions of Christians, having learned to know the love of God in Christ, have learned to throw their entire weight on God, trusting that "underneath are the everlasting arms." Into His hands they commit all of their *yesterdays*—knowing that in His mercy He will forgive them. Into His hands they commit *today*—knowing that it is another day of grace. And into His hands they commit all of their *tomorrows*—knowing that all of His mercies that have been "new every morning" will be just as new, just as sure, and just as all-sufficing tomorrow as they are today. Theirs is the peace of a life that is "hidden with Christ in God."

That is why I say Jesus is my Peace.

In the cross of Christ I glory,
  Tow'ring o'er the wrecks of time.
All the light of sacred story
  Gathers round its head sublime.

When the woes of life o'ertake me,
  Hopes deceive, and fears annoy,
Never shall the cross forsake me;
  Lo, it glows with peace and joy.

When the sun of bliss is beaming
  Light and love upon my way,
From the cross the radiance streaming
  Adds more luster to the day.

Bane and blessing, pain and pleasure
  By the cross are sanctified;
Peace is there that knows no measure,
  Joys that through all time abide.

Power

A mother visited her boy at college. Upon entering his room, her eye swept across the walls, which were covered with more than a dozen suggestive pictures. Her heart was grieved, but she said nothing.

Several days later, the mailman delivered a package to the young man. It was a gift from his mother— a beautifully framed picture of the head of Christ.

Proudly the boy hung the picture on the wall above his desk. That night before he went to bed, he removed the picture that hung closest to the face of Christ. The next day another picture was consigned to the wastebasket. Day after day, the pictures began to disappear from the walls until only one remained—the picture of the Savior.

No one had lectured to the boy, no one had told him to remove the other pictures. The power of the contemplation of Christ had made it impossible for him to keep the other pictures on his walls.

Christ *is* like that! His is the power of heaven. Once a man has found his salvation in the blood of Jesus Christ, he will find the power of Christ *expelling* the evil from his heart and *propelling* him to deeds of Christian love and virtue. The power to fight sin and the power to do right are gifts that Christ bestows on all believers.

But we must belong to Christ before we can lay claim to that power. He says, "As the branch cannot bear fruit by itself, unless it abides in the vine, neither can you, unless you abide in Me. I am the vine; you are the branches. Whoever abides in Me and I in him, he it is that bears much fruit, for apart from Me you can do nothing." Only he who clings to Christ by a living faith will have the power to resist sin, to overcome temptation, and to lead a life of Christian goodness. Outside of the vine—severed from the only source of spiritual life—there is no spiritual power. "Apart from Me you can do nothing."

The apostle Paul, who was transformed from a spiritual weakling into one of the world's spiritual giants, made no secret of the source of his power. "I can do all things through Him who strengthens me," he says. And in another place he writes, "It is no longer I who live, but Christ who lives in me. And the life I now live in the flesh I live by faith in the Son of God, who loved me and gave Himself for me."

Where did Paul get the power to stop in his tracks, to put an end to his worthless career, to lead a life of charity and decency, to stand up under the ridicule and opposition of his countrymen, to endure beating and stoning and bitter persecution, to sing hymns of praise in prison, and finally to give his life in payment for his faith? Where did he find this power to endure and to achieve? "I can do all things through Him who strengthens me," he says. "It is no longer I who live, but Christ who lives in

me." Surely, if anyone had asked Paul what Jesus
meant to him, he would have answered, "Among
the many other things that Jesus means to me,
He means power—power to overcome evil,
power to endure, power to gain a continuing
victory."

I, too, have found Christ to be my inex-
haustible Source of spiritual and moral power.
In moments of temptation, in the hour of trial,
in days of doubt and darkness, I have fled to
"Jesus, lover of my soul," with the prayer:

> *Reach me out Thy gracious hand!*
> *While I of Thy strength receive.*

And without fail I have received His strength:
strength to stand in the midst of the tempest,
strength to outlast the storm, strength to bear
the burden of the cross, strength to resist the
onslaught of sin—or, having fallen, to tread the
path of the prodigal back to the Father's house
and to be assured of full and free forgiveness.
These victories were by no means mine. Left to
myself, to my own puny powers of resistance or

endurance, I would have succumbed long since. "Not that we are sufficient in ourselves . . . our sufficiency is from God." "But by the grace of God I am what I am." These confessions of the penitent apostle are also mine.

To receive power from Christ I must, of course, believe in Him. I must see in Him the eternal Son of God, my Savior, my ever-present Friend. Paul was a man. He is dead. He cannot help me. Peter, James, and John were men. They are dead. They cannot help me. But Christ is the eternal Son of God, the almighty Creator and Sustainer of the universe. By His resurrection from the dead, He has proved Himself to be the Father's only Son, who lives and reigns with Him in highest heaven. He "was declared to be the Son of God in power . . . by His resurrection from the dead," says Paul. And at another place, the Scriptures say of Him, "He upholds the universe by the word of His power." With Him all things are possible, for He Himself has said, "All authority in heaven and on earth has been given to Me." And now in that power I am privileged to share.

But how do I make application for my share of that power? How is this strength poured into my weakness? How do I make contact? I receive power from Christ by believing. I accept the helping hand of Christ by simply trusting Him. He has promised me pardon for my sin, peace for my soul, strength in the hour of trouble, courage in the face of difficulty, power in the moment of temptation—and I receive this pardon, peace, and power simply by trusting that He will keep His promise.

> *I am trusting Thee, Lord Jesus,*
>   *Trusting only Thee;*
> *Trusting Thee for full salvation,*
>   *Great and free.*
>
> *I am trusting Thee for power,*
>   *Thine can never fail.*
> *Words which Thou Thyself shalt give me*
>   *Must prevail.*

I seek daily reassurance of His power through prayer. More than once, when the burden seemed too heavy, when the assignment seemed too great, when my shoulders seemed too weak to bear the burden, I have called upon Him; and always either He has lightened the burden to match my strength, or He has increased my strength to match the burden. And in His power, I have prevailed.

Perhaps the best illustration of the power of Christ resting upon those who believe in Him is given us in the lives of His disciples. If ever there was a band of defeated, dejected, and frightened men, it was the little group of eleven whose world collapsed when their Master died. Like frightened sheep, they were huddled in a back room on a side street in the city of Jerusalem—weak, timid, quaking, afraid of their own shadows!

But what a difference when once they had been assured of their Lord's resurrection from the dead! He lives! He lives! He is not dead! He is with us, as He promised! The knowledge that their dearest friend was alive again transformed a lonely, empty world into a world that was

charged with the power of His presence. No
matter where they went from that time on, they
knew that the omnipresent Christ was with
them. No combination of hell or world could
successfully withstand them. They had become
conscious of a tremendous power hitherto
unknown to them: the power of the helping
Christ.

And so they went forth to live courageous
and victorious lives. Peter, the weakling who
had deserted his Lord in His moment of utmost
need, all of a sudden becomes a bold preacher
of the Word. Stephen stands like a pillar and
is unafraid. John preaches boldly in the temple.
And Saul of Tarsus sets out to turn the world
upside down for Christ. "You will receive
power," Christ had told them. Now they had
received that power.

And down through the centuries the pages
of history are filled with the names of men
and women who have overcome the world in
the power of Christ. Millions upon millions
have confessed Christ to be the source of their

spiritual power and have come to Christ again and again with the humble prayer of Charles Wesley:

Jesus, my Truth, my Way,
*   My sure, unerring Light,*
On Thee my feeble soul I stay,
*   Which Thou wilt lead aright.*

Thou seest my feebleness;
*   Jesus, be Thou my Pow'r,*
My Help and Refuge in distress,
*   My Fortress and my Tow'r.*

Give me to trust in Thee;
*   Be Thou my sure Abode;*
My Horn and Rock and Buckler be,
*   My Savior and my God.*

Myself I cannot save,
*   Myself I cannot keep;*
But strength in Thee I surely have,
*   Whose eyelids never sleep.*

My soul to Thee alone
  Now, therefore, I commend.
Thou, Jesus, having loved Thine own,
  Wilt love me to the end.

What does Jesus mean to me? What did He mean to the faithful few whom He sent out to preach His Gospel? What did He mean to the millions who have lived and died in devotion to His name? Among many other things, He has meant *power*—power to resist sin; power to lead the fuller, happier life; power to bear the burdens of each day; power to achieve the final victory. "To all who did receive Him, who believed in His name, He gave the right to become children of God."

Provision

The story is told of a man who invited a few friends to a most unusual dinner. As the guests entered the dining room, they noticed a silver screen at one end of the spacious room and a projector at the other. Before the oysters were served, the light went out, and there upon the screen they saw men toiling in the sea and among the rocks, in the cold mist, dredging for the oysters they were to eat.

When the vegetables came, they saw a picture of little children who should have been in school or at play, but instead were shelling peas in a distant canning factory. When the bread was brought in, they were shown pictures of plowing and harrowing and sowing and reaping and threshing and grinding—the

45

infinite labor and pains that were necessary before that bread could come to them. The meat was served, and they beheld the hard life of the men on the plains and in the stockyards and on the railroads, all of which was necessary before those dainty and delicious portions of meat could be theirs.

When they had finished, they knew, as they had never known before, the sacrifice of toil and time on the part of others that lies behind the common things in life. Unfortunately, the demonstration, as good as it was, was not complete. For had the host thought just one step farther, he would have finished his visual demonstration with a picture of the Savior with hands raised in blessing, and on the screen he would have thrown the well-known verse of Scripture,

"The eyes of all look to You, and You give them their food in due season.

> *You open your hand;*
> *You satisfy the desire of every living*
> *thing."*

It is Jesus, the Christ, the omnipotent Son of God, who provides all mankind with daily food. Speaking of Jesus, the Bible says, "All things were made through Him, and without Him was not any thing made that was made." Paul writes to the Ephesians, praising the almighty God, "who created all things." And to the Colossians, the same apostle extols the almighty power of Christ, who is "the image of the invisible God, the firstborn of all creation. For by Him all things were created, in heaven and on earth." In other words, Jesus Christ, together with the Father and the Holy Spirit, is the Creator of the universe. And not only the Creator, but also the Sustainer, for the Bible says of Him, "He upholds the universe by the word of His power."

I have found in Jesus Christ my great

Provider, who cares for all my needs, both temporal and spiritual. Writing about God's great providence, Martin Luther included the following lines in the Small Catechism, which he wrote for the children of his day, more than four hundred years ago,

"I believe that God has made me and all creatures; that He has given me my body and soul, eyes, ears, and all my members, my reason and all my senses, and still takes care of them. He also gives me clothing and shoes, food and drink, house and home, wife and children, land, animals, and all I have. He richly and daily provides me with all that I need to support this body and life. He defends me against all danger and guards and protects me from all evil. All this He does only out of fatherly, divine goodness and mercy, without any merit or worthiness in me. For all this it is my duty to thank and praise, serve and obey Him. This is most certainly true."

Yes, this is most certainly true. But it is true only because God has become my Father through Jesus Christ. "For in Christ Jesus you are all sons of God, through faith," the Bible tells us. I am assured of God's love and providence only because Jesus, by His suffering and death, has restored me to sonship with the Father. It is true, in a certain sense, that the unbelieving children of the world receive the same temporal blessings that God bestows upon His children. "He makes His sun rise on the evil and on the good, and sends rain on the just and on the unjust." But their relationship to God is not that of Father and child; theirs is not the loving confidence that a loving son has toward his father; theirs is merely the helpless dependence of a creature upon his Creator. And that makes all the difference in the world!

A Roman emperor, after a brilliant military campaign, was returning in triumph to Rome. Kings and princes were chained to his chariot wheels as trophies of his triumph. Cheering crowds filled the city streets to pay homage to the conquering hero. As the spectacular procession

passed through the city's center thoroughfare,
a little girl, wild with joy, dashed toward the
moving chariot. The strong arm of a uniformed
guard stopped her. "That is the chariot of the
emperor," he said. "You must not try to touch it."
The little one replied, "He may be your emperor,
but he is *my father!*" A moment later she was
not only in the chariot but clasped fondly in her
father's arms. Even so it is with those who have
come to God through Christ. While God is the
Emperor of all men, He is that and infinitely
more to those who accept His Son as Savior;
He is their Father!

And as their Father, He is moved by love to
provide for all of their necessities. It is true, His
Father-love may find it necessary to withhold
some physical blessings from His children. But
the hand that withholds is attached to the heart
that loves, and that is all we need to know. One
of the most beautiful passages of the Bible is
that section of the Sermon on the Mount where
Jesus speaks movingly to His disciples about the

tender care of His Father for all His children. "Do not be anxious about your life, what you will eat or what you will drink, nor about your body, what you will put on. Is not life more than food, and the body more than clothing? Look at the birds of the air: they neither sow nor reap nor gather into barns, and yet your heavenly Father feeds them. Are you not of more value than they? And which of you by being anxious can add a single hour to his span of life? And why are you anxious about clothing? Consider the lilies of the field, how they grow: they neither toil nor spin, yet I tell you, even Solomon in all his glory was not arrayed like one of these. But if God so clothes the grass of the field, which today is alive and tomorrow is thrown into the oven, will He not much more clothe you, O you of little faith? Therefore do not be anxious, saying, 'What shall we eat?' or 'What shall we drink?' or 'What shall we wear?' For the Gentiles seek after all these things, and your heavenly Father knows that you need them all. But seek first the kingdom of God and His righteousness, and all these things will be added to you."

"Your Father!" What a tender, reassuring touch these words give to the promise of the Savior! "Your heavenly Father knows that you need them all." The weary child at the end of day will often confide his wants and needs to his earthly father and then drift off to peaceful slumber. It is enough that Father knows! His love will find a way. His love will contrive the means to satisfy tomorrow's needs.

Our heavenly Father does know our every want and wish. And He is abundantly able and willing to provide. "He who did not spare His own Son but gave Him up for us all, how will He not also with Him graciously give us all things?" There is no need in our life, however great or small, that God does not know and which He will not fill if it be necessary for our temporal and eternal happiness. "My God will supply every need of yours according to His riches in glory in Christ Jesus," says Paul.

But will He? Can I trust Him? Can I be sure that each succeeding day will find a sufficient measure of His grace and goodness to see me and my loved ones through? Yes, I can be sure. John, in his Gospel, speaks of the heavenly glory of Jesus and says, "From His fullness we have all received, grace upon grace." Christ's goodness pours in upon us as the waves of the sea. As the one comes, there is always another close behind, and then another and another. Christ's capacity and willingness to provide are unlimited and eternal.

A wealthy man died and left instructions to his wife to give a certain portion of his fortune to a poor minister who had frequently remembered the family with deeds of kindness. The widow thought it would be best to turn the money over to the minister in regular installments, so she mailed him $25, and inside the envelope she placed a little slip of paper upon which was written, "More to follow." Every week, without fail, the elderly man would find a package of money in his mailbox with the identical message, "More to follow."

"More to follow!" That is Christ's unbreakable pledge to all who believe in Him. The blessings that we receive today are but a pledge of those that we shall receive tomorrow; and those we receive tomorrow will bear the pledge of heaven, "More to follow." His mercies are new every morning. His compassions fail not.

The psalmist writes, "I have been young, and now am old, yet I have not seen the righteous forsaken or his children begging for bread." He who could feed five thousand people with "five barley loaves and two fish" is still capable of supporting those who trust in Him. His multiplying hand has never lost its power. Jesus says, "I am the good shepherd." The believer says, "The LORD is my shepherd; I shall not want." He daily supplies me with rich provision. I need not fear for tomorrow's needs, for He has promised to supply them. The Bible assures the believer, "Godliness is of value in every way, as it holds promise for the present life and also for the life to come." Christ has promised to take care also of the bodily needs of those who come to God by Him.

I have found Christ to be my heavenly Provider. Since I have accepted Him as Savior and Sovereign of my life, I have entrusted Him also with the provision of my physical necessities. I have endeavored, with the help of God, to live up to the scriptural pattern: "casting all your anxieties on Him, because He cares for you." And I have found Him supremely able and willing to provide.

> *Savior, I follow on,*
> *Guided by Thee,*
> *Seeing not yet the hand*
> *That leadeth me.*
> *Hushed be my heart and still,*
> *Fear I no further ill,*
> *Only to meet Thy will*
> *My will shall be.*

Riven the rock for me
    Thirst to relieve,
Manna from heaven falls
Fresh ev'ry eve.
    Never a want severe
Causeth my eye a tear
But Thou dost whisper near,
    "Only believe."

Savior, I long to walk
    Closer with Thee;
Led by Thy guiding hand,
    Ever to be
Constantly near Thy side,
Quickened and purified,
Living for Him who died
    Freely for me.

Companionship

There come moments into the life of every one of us when the world seems to pass us by and we are forced to eat the bread of loneliness. The rich and the poor, the mighty and the weak, the dweller in the palace and the tenant in the shack—all have felt at some time or another the piercing pang that comes with the knowledge of being unnoticed, unneeded, or unwanted.

Perhaps no pain is more poignant than the sharp and sudden realization that our friends have found us to be "expendable," that, while the march of life is passing by our door, we have been left to sit alone. The human heart cries out against the aching pain of loneliness. And its cries can never be completely silenced until it has found the solace and the strength that come from true companionship.

I have found that true Companion—in Christ!

Scarcely an hour passes without my being clearly conscious of His presence. Morning, noon, and night I know that He is with me. Again and again I find myself in earnest conversation, sharing with Him my problems and perplexities, seeking guidance and direction. In the midst of a busy day, I find myself telling Him about my joys, sharing with Him my triumphs, and speaking to Him in tones of gratitude for blessings without number. And in each case, the very assurance of His presence and His interest in my joys and sorrows pours new life, new courage, and new gladness into my soul.

But can I be sure that He is there? Can I be sure that He is with me and that He can hear the flood of thoughts that I have never uttered? Yes, I *can* be sure. This intimate companionship between the Savior and the individual believer is one of the most beautiful assurances of the Bible.

While He was still on earth, Jesus spoke fondly and frequently about this close companionship that was to exist between Him and every man who would put his trust in Him.

During the closing days of His life, this fellowship seemed to be uppermost in all His thinking. Again and again He assured His followers that even after His death (yes, *especially* after His death and resurrection and ascension into heaven) He would be united with them in the closest fellowship the world has ever known. "My sheep hear My voice," He said, "I know them, and they follow Me. I give them eternal life, and they will never perish, and no one will snatch them out of My hand."

A little later He assured His followers: "In that day you will know that I am in My Father, and you in Me, and I in you." And again: "I am the vine; you are the branches. Whoever abides in Me and I in him, he it is that bears much fruit." Not many hours before His crucifixion, He prayed to His heavenly Father, pleading for those who believed in Him: "That they may be one even as We are one, I in them and You in Me." And finally, just before He ascended visibly into heaven, He gave the ultimate assurance to all Christians of all times: "Behold, I am with you always, to the end of the age." Christ is the heaven-sent Companion to every heart that puts its trust in Him.

It is comforting beyond measure to see how the Bible abounds in assurances of God's presence in the lives of individual believers. "I will never leave you nor forsake you." "My presence will go with you." "Fear not, for I am with you; be not dismayed, for I am your God; I will strengthen you, I will help you, I will uphold you with My righteous right hand." "I will be with you. I will not leave you or forsake you. Be strong and courageous." The companionship of the individual believer with his God and Savior is a companionship based upon the faithful pledges of an eternal Friend.

Jesus, Thou art mine forever,
Dearer far than earth to me;

Neither life nor death shall sever
Those sweet ties which bind to Thee.

All were drear to me and lonely
If Thy presence gladdened not;
While I sing to Thee, Thee only,
Mine's an ever blissful lot.

Jesus, Thou art mine forever;
Never suffer me to stray;
Let me in my weakness never
Cast my priceless pearl away.

I was brought into this intimate companionship with Christ through the covenant of Baptism. "For as many of you as were baptized into Christ have put on Christ." This intimate fellowship with Christ is strengthened by my frequent presence at His Supper. There in an unspeakably sublime manner He draws near to me and assures me of His loving presence, His abundant pardon, and His mighty power. "Take, eat; this is My body. . . . Drink of it, all of you, for this is My blood." "Do this in remembrance of Me." I attend His

Holy Supper frequently for the strengthening of my faith, for the reassurance of my fellowship with Him, and for renewed power to lead an ever better Christian life.

But in Christ I have also found a larger fellowship. I have been united in the bonds of spiritual companionship with millions of fellow Christians, both those now living and those who long since have gone to join the Savior. "Because there is one bread, we who are many are one body, for we all partake of the one bread," says Paul. The name of Jesus unites more people than does any other name. I have a sense of kinship, a sense of fellowship, not only with the prophets and apostles, not only with martyrs and the saints of all the ages, but with scores and hundreds of thousands of like-minded people in my own denomination, and with uncounted millions of believers in every quarter of the globe. For, "we, though many, are one body in Christ, and individually members one of another," says the apostle. That is why Paul, writing to the handful of Christians in the city of Ephesus, could say, "So then you are no longer strangers and aliens, but you are fellow citizens with the saints and members of the household of God." They were no longer alone; they had been accepted into the family of God, and their brethren and sisters in the faith were more numerous than they had ever dreamed.

I, too, have been accepted into the family of God through faith in Jesus Christ. I, too, share in the comfort and strength that comes from the knowledge that millions of my fellow men are my brethren and sisters in Christ and that we who believe in Christ are the children of one Father. It was this blessed assurance that inspired John Fawcett to write the lines of the beautiful hymn:

> *Blest be the tie that binds*
> *Our hearts in Christian love;*
> *The fellowship of kindred minds*
> *Is like to that above.*
>
> *Before our Father's throne*
> *We pour our ardent prayers;*

Our fears, our hopes, our aims are one,
Our comforts and our cares.

From sorrow, toil, and pain,
And sin we shall be free
And perfect love and friendship reign
Through all eternity.

Through Christ I am walking through the world hand in hand with the greatest, the highest, and the noblest names of history. What illustrious company! Through Christ I am walking through the world hand in hand with those people who are doing the best, the finest, and the loveliest things in the world today. What glorious companionship! Through Christ I have become a part of that family to which the world owes everything that it has received from two thousand years of Christian influence. What splendid fellowship! Through Christ I have joined hands with those people of whom the Savior says: "You are the salt of the earth. . . . You are the light of the world." What a sublime association!

Alone? Lonely? Yes, sometimes it may seem so. But I am never really alone. In Christ I have a true Companion, a Friend that never fails. And through faith in His redemption, I have become one of the "fellow citizens with the saints and members of the household of God." Who could ask for better company?

And so, if you ask me, "What does Jesus mean to you?" I answer, "Jesus means many things to me. One of them is *companionship*, true and constant—*fellowship*, intimate and sure."

Hope

A missionary to South Africa told an interesting story. In the course of his travels, he was called upon to make a long journey with Cecil Rhodes, perhaps the most influential of the British leaders in that country. The missionary was struck by the depression and gloom that seemed to surround this otherwise great man. One day he gathered sufficient courage to put the point-blank question, "Mr. Rhodes, are you a happy man?"

"I shall never forget," the missionary goes on to report, "how he threw himself back against the cushions and, gripping the arm of the seat, exclaimed, while looking at me in a tense attitude, 'Happy? I—happy? No, indeed!' After a while I said to him: 'Mr. Rhodes, there is only one place where we can find real happiness, and that is down at the feet of the crucified Savior, because only there can we be freed from our sins.' After some time Mr. Rhodes said to me slowly and emphatically, 'I would give all that I possess if I could believe what you believe!'"

Mr. Rhodes had money, friends, power, fame, and whatever else this world may offer any person. He lived in a lovely home and was highly respected by thousands. But he had not found happiness, because he had not found hope. He had not been assured of a future that would bring him those things that his heart lacked most—peace, joy, assurance, the confident prospect of eternal bliss and glory.

Those things are to be found only in Christ. Nowhere else in this whole wide world can men find any foundation on which to build their hopes. They have tried it, but always they have failed. During the prosperous years following the First World War, millions placed their hope in bulging bank accounts, only to eat the ashes of disillusionment when these bank accounts disappeared in the crash of 1929. During the thirties, men placed their hope in their own cleverness and in their own ability to achieve a more abundant life, but the wan faces of agonized millions and the gutted ruins of a continent that boasted of its culture and accomplishments bear silent testimony to the *misplaced* hopes of a generation that was tragically misled.

Only in Christ is there hope, because only in Christ can men find the solution of their deepest needs. It is remarkable how the Bible identifies the entire Christian hope with the person and work of Christ. The apostle Paul, for instance, after he had told the Christians at Rome all about the forgiveness that was theirs through faith in Jesus Christ, continued by saying, "Therefore, since we have been justified by faith, we have peace with God through our Lord Jesus Christ. Through Him we have also obtained access by faith into this grace in which we stand, and we rejoice in hope of the glory of God. More than that, we rejoice in our sufferings, knowing that suffering produces endurance, and endurance produces character, and character produces hope, and hope does not put us to shame, because God's love has been poured into our hearts through the Holy Spirit who has been given to us." All of Paul's hope for the future was wrapped up in what he had found in Christ. He had found forgiveness and peace in Christ, and he had been assured that this forgiveness and peace had been given to him as his priceless and permanent possession. With these in his heart *to stay*, he had found a sure foundation for his hope.

> *My hope is built on nothing less*
> *Than Jesus' blood and righteousness;*
> *No merit of my own I claim*
> *But wholly lean on Jesus' name.*
> *On Christ, the solid rock, I stand;*
> *All other ground is sinking sand.*

It is noteworthy how often the New Testament speaks of the hope of the Christian, "the hope of the gospel," the "hope in the promise," "the hope to which He has called you," "the hope laid up for you in heaven," "the hope of glory," "hope in our Lord Jesus Christ," "our blessed hope," "the hope of eternal life," "the full assurance of hope," the hope we have "as a sure and steadfast anchor," "a living hope," and scores of other passages. And when the New Testament writers use the word *hope* in connection with the future of the child of God, they use it not in the sense of a pious wish, but in the sense of a sure confidence. The Christian's hope, since it is rooted in the person and promises of Jesus Christ, is a "hope [that] does not put us to shame," a hope that is as sure as Christ Himself is sure.

But what does this mean to me? It means that inasmuch as I am a child of God through faith in Jesus Christ, the future holds more good for me than I could ever hope for. Christ is my guarantee of a blessed future. If God saw fit to send His only Son into the world to suffer and to die that I might live, and if in His mercy He has brought me to faith in Jesus as my Savior, the worst that could ever happen to me is *past,* and the best that can ever happen to me still lies in the future. This is what Scripture means when it says, "He who did not spare His own Son but gave Him up for us all, how will He not also with Him graciously give us all things?" It was this hope of which Paul spoke when he wrote to his young pupil Titus, "He saved us ... according to His own mercy ... that being justified by His grace we might become heirs according to the hope of eternal life." As a child of God, through Christ, I am an heir of heaven. Eternal life, an unspeakably better life than that which I now am living, is my heritage. And I can live in the daily prospect of that better life!

All this is what I mean when I say that Jesus is my *Hope.* His presence will brighten every foot of the path that stretches out before me. His promise will uphold me, no matter what may still confront me. His power will be my stay in every evil hour. The assurance that I am His and He is mine is my pledge of eternal life with Him in glory. What a blessed prospect! What a blessed hope!

When with sorrow I am stricken,
  Hope anew my heart will quicken;
All my longing shall be stilled.
  To His loving-kindness tender
Soul and body I surrender,
  For on God alone I build.

Well He knows what best to grant me;
  All the longing hopes that haunt me,
Joy and sorrow, have their day.
  I shall doubt His wisdom never;
As God wills, so be it ever;
  I commit to Him my way.

If my days on earth He lengthen,
  God my weary soul will strengthen;
All my trust in Him I place.
  Earthly wealth is not abiding,
Like a stream away is gliding;
  Safe I anchor in His grace.

Truth

One of the deepest cravings of the human heart is to know the truth. The anxious mother's heart would give anything to know the truth about her wayward child. The lover is hungry for the truth of his beloved. The worried family tosses restlessly on sleepless pillows because it does not know the truth about a parent, son or daughter, brother or sister who has been reported missing from the field of battle. If only they knew *the truth*, there would be an end to this agony of uncertainty.

But a far deeper hunger for the truth is gnawing at the heart of every man and woman. Even the person who professes to have no religion at all will confess in his honest moments that he is troubled by a torturing uncertainty. In the presence of others, he may boast that he can get along without a faith in God. He may even proudly assert that there is no God. In his secret heart of hearts, however, he cannot suppress the haunting question: *But what if there is a God?*

If there is a God, what kind of God is He? What does He think of me? What does He intend to do with me? How do I fit into His plans for the universe, particularly His plans for the human family? What is my personal relationship to Him—and His to me?

Whether a man lives in Chicago, Cleveland, or New York, in Johannesburg, Buenos Aires, or Beijing, he is distressingly conscious of a hunger for the truth about these questions.

And what about a life beyond the grave? Will there be a resurrection? If so, what is to become of me? Will my destiny in the life to come be determined by what I do today? Am I at this moment forging the shackles that will imprison my soul and body in all eternity? Is there a hell? If so, how can I escape it? Is there a heaven? If so, how can I be assured that someday I shall be there? These are questions that have troubled the heart of man down through the ages. And they demand nothing less than *the truth* as their reply.

Furthermore, how am I to get rhyme or reason out of the life I now am living? I eat, I work, I sleep, I awake—I repeat the same process day after day and year after year. But why? For what purpose? Just to wear out and be discarded as a suit of old clothes? Just to move on and make room for others? How am I to fit all the puzzling pieces of my life into a sensible and purposeful pattern—my unemployment, my hospital bills, my bitter disappointments, my failures, my heartaches? Why must these things be? Is there an intelligent plan that lies behind them all and that can give them meaning? I want to know the truth.

I know that men have given answers to all these questions. Philosophers have crowded our libraries with learned books on just these subjects. They have spun impressive theories. But what I need as the polestar of my life—my guide, my chart, my compass—is not a theory that has been invented by a man who is just as subject to error as I am. No, I need the truth— *God's truth.*

I have found that truth—in Jesus.

I have placed my trust in the words of Christ, first of all, because God Himself has told me that the words of Christ are trustworthy. Fifteen hundred years before the birth of Jesus, God spoke to His people through the prophet Moses and said, "The LORD your God will raise up for you a prophet like me from among you . . . it is to Him you shall listen." Some fifteen hundred years later, after the ascension of the Savior into heaven, Peter addressed an unbelieving multitude and told them that this prophecy had been fulfilled in Jesus. "Moses said, 'The Lord God will raise up for you a prophet like me from your brothers. You shall listen to Him in whatever He tells you." In other words, God has told me that I am to listen to His Son "in whatever He tells" me. And so I look to Jesus for the truth.

But more. God the Father placed His stamp

of divine approval on His Son and on His teachings both at the occasion of the Savior's Baptism and again on the Mount of Transfiguration. At the Baptism of our Lord, we are told, the Father spoke from heaven, saying, "This is My beloved Son, with whom I am well pleased." On the Mount of Transfiguration, we are told, the Savior's face "shone like the sun, and His clothes became white as light," and the Father again spoke from heaven, saying, "This is My beloved Son, with whom I am well pleased; listen to Him!"

Jesus, then, is no mere prophet among many prophets, no mere teacher among many teachers, no mere voice among many voices. He is, by the testimony of God Himself, *the* Teacher. He is the only Voice of God to man. "Listen to Him!" Surely, a Prophet with those credentials will know the truth. And He will speak the truth. I accept the words of Christ as truth, then, because God Himself has vouched for the truthfulness of His own beloved Son.

I place my trust in the words of Christ,

furthermore, because Christ with His own lips has assured me that His Gospel is the truth. "If you abide in My word," He says, "you are truly My disciples, and you will know the truth, and the truth will set you free." To Pilate's question, "So you are a king?" Jesus replied, knowing that in a matter of hours He would be nailed to a cross, "You say that I am a king. For this purpose I was born and for this purpose I have come into the world—to bear witness to the truth. Everyone who is of the truth listens to My voice."

To the unbelieving people of His day, Jesus said, "I am the light of the world. Whoever follows Me will not walk in darkness, but will have the light of life." And shortly before His death, He assured His sorrowing disciples, "I am the way, and the truth, and the life. No one comes to the Father except through Me." He not only knows the truth, He not only has the truth, He not only brings the truth: He is Truth. He is the Truth of heaven come down to earth. In Him the stumbling, groping mind of man finds the answer to the deepest problems of the soul.

I place my trust in the words of Christ, finally, because the whole Bible is nothing but one chorus of testimony to the heavenly wisdom of the Savior. To the holy writers, Jesus is God's truth come down from heaven. In Him "are hidden all the treasures of wisdom and knowledge," the Bible tells us. "In Him the whole fullness of deity dwells bodily." John, the disciple whom Jesus loved, opens his Gospel with the well-known words, "In the beginning was the Word [Jesus], and the Word was with God, and the Word was God.... And the Word became flesh and dwelt among us, and we have seen His glory, glory as of the only Son from the Father, full of grace and truth." To John and to the other Bible writers, Christ was the Word of God, the Word become flesh, "full of grace and truth."

> *O Word of God incarnate,*
> *O Wisdom from on high,*

O Truth unchanged, unchanging,
O Light of our dark sky:

In a day such as ours, when "darkness shall cover the earth, and thick darkness the peoples," when men's hearts are failing them for fear, when the hope of ever coming to the knowledge of the truth in spiritual matters is gradually being given up as vain and futile, Christ is still mankind's only hope. He is still the light of the world. He is still the way. He is still the truth.

There are millions on this earth whose problems have been solved in the light of the Gospel of Christ. To them He has become the heavenly Counselor of whom Isaiah prophesied when he looked forward seven hundred years to that first Christmas night and exclaimed: "To us a child is born, to us a son is given; and the government shall be upon His shoulder, and His name shall be called Wonderful Counselor, Mighty God, Everlasting Father, Prince of Peace."

Christ has been my counselor. In Him my life has been given meaning. In Him I have found the answers to those problems of the soul that cry out in the night for an answer. In Him I have found the truth: the truth about God, the truth about man, the truth about life, the truth about death, the truth about heaven, the truth about hell.

From Him and the sacred pages of His Word, I have learned the truth about the origin and destiny of man. I have learned that man is a creature richly endowed and gifted by God but ruined because of voluntary sin. I have learned that man, as far as his natural abilities are concerned, is utterly corrupt, completely helpless, and—if left to himself—doomed to an eternal separation from his Maker.

But I have also learned from Christ that God in His mercy has intervened on my behalf. He has sent His only Son into the world to pay the penalty of mankind's guilt, to effect a reconciliation between the Father and His wayward children, and to win a complete redemption for every member of the human family. To achieve this indescribable salvation,

Jesus was born, suffered, died, and rose again.

From Christ I have also learned the meaning and purpose of life. I am no longer baffled by its evils, its disappointments, and its heartaches. While there are still many pieces that I am not yet able to fit into the pattern, He has shown me the completed picture and has assured me that every piece has its allotted place in the pattern He has planned. By His suffering and death for my redemption, He has given me an overwhelming demonstration of His and His Father's love for me. Assured of *that* love, I can rest assured of His continued guidance and protection. "We know that for those who love God all things work together for good, for those who are called according to His purpose." "He who did not spare His own Son but gave Him up for us all, how will He not also with Him graciously give us all things?" These are truths that He has given me. These are truths I trust, and knowing these, I am content.

From Christ I have learned that for me there lies at the end of the road a happy Father's house. "In My Father's house," He assures me, "are many rooms. . . . I go to prepare a place for you. . . . I will come again and will take you to Myself, that where I am you may be also. And you know the way. . . . I am the way, and the truth, and the life. No one comes to the Father except through Me." Since I know what lies at the end of the road, the heat of the journey that lies between will not discourage or dismay me.

These are the truths that have been given me, not by any man, but by God Himself. They have been given me by Him of whom the Father said, "This is My beloved Son. . . . listen to Him." I have heard them from the lips of Him who said, "If you abide in My word . . . you will know the truth." I have been assured of these things by Him whom the Scriptures call "the Word of God," and "the Word [become] flesh." I have been taught these things by Him of whom the Bible says: In Him "are hidden all the treasures of wisdom and knowledge." I have been told these things by Him who says, "I am . . . the truth"!

And so, if you ask what Jesus means to me, I

answer: To me Jesus is the truth, heaven's eternal truth, God's truth to man, the only truth by which a man can set his course and be assured of an eternal destiny of bliss and glory!

> *You are the way; through You alone*
> *Can we the Father find;*
> *In You, O Christ, has God revealed*
> *His heart and will and mind.*
>
> *You are the truth; Your Word alone*
> *True wisdom can impart;*
> *You only can inform the mind*
> *And purify the heart.*
>
> *You are the life; the empty tomb*
> *Proclaims Your conqu'ring arm,*
> *And those who put their trust in You*
> *Not death nor hell shall harm.*
>
> *You are the way, the truth, the life;*
> *Grant us that way to know,*
> *That truth to keep, that life to win*
> *Whose joys eternal flow.*

Assurance

In the early days of our country, a weary traveler came to the banks of the Mississippi for the first time. There was no bridge by which he could cross. It was early winter, and the surface of the mighty stream was covered with ice. Could he *dare* cross over? Would the uncertain ice be able to bear his weight?

Night was falling, and it was urgent that he reach the other side. Finally, after much hesitation and with many fears, he began to creep cautiously across the surface of the ice on his hands and knees. He thought that by doing so he might distribute his weight as much as possible and keep the ice from breaking under his heavy load.

About halfway over, he heard the sound of singing behind him. Out of the dusk there came a workman, driving a four-horse load of coal across the ice and singing merrily as he went his carefree way!

Here was the first man—on his knees, trembling for fear that the ice might not be strong enough to bear him up! And there, as if whisked away by the winter's wind, went the workman, his horses, his sleigh, and his load of coal—upheld by the same ice on which the first man was creeping! The workman had gone that way before; he had tested the ice and he knew that it was well able to carry him and his load safely to the other side.

I have tested Christ. In every scene of life—in joy and sorrow, in success and failure, in health and sickness, in moments of crisis "when every earthly prop gave way"—I have trusted Christ and have found that He was able to carry both me and my burden and bring me safely to the other side. With Paul and with believers of all the ages, I can say: "I know whom I have believed, and I am convinced that He is able to guard until that Day what has been entrusted to me." I know the ice won't break!

And this assurance is no mere whistling in the dark, no mere pleasant journey in the land of make-believe. It is firmly rooted in the unshakable promises of an unshakable book, in the sacred pledge of the world's most sacred person, and in the experience of millions who can attest to His faithfulness in carrying out His pledge.

But what are the assurances that the Bible gives to those who have come to God through Christ? One of the most beautiful as well as one of the most meaningful Bible assurances is the memorable word of Moses, "The eternal God is your dwelling place, and underneath are the everlasting arms." The story is told of a mother eagle that built her nest on a ledge of rock that jutted precariously over a tremendous precipice. Soaring through the air one day on her return to her nest, she was startled at the sight of her baby eagle struggling on the jagged edge of the rock, trying to prevent a fall that was sure to crush its body at the bottom of the canyon. Unable to get to the ledge before her little one would fall, the mother eagle with the speed of lightning swooped low beneath the jutting rock, spread her strong wings to break the fall of her darling, and with her precious cargo clinging to the feathers of her mighty wing, glided safely to the canyon's floor. "The eternal God is your dwelling place, and underneath are the everlasting arms."

Those who have come to God through faith in Christ have found again and again that—no matter how acute the danger, how severe the crisis, or how piercing the pain—"underneath are the everlasting arms."

This assurance of the love of God through Christ—a love that not only pardons our sins and thus gives us peace and hope, but a love that goes with us in our daily lives and surrounds us with protecting walls of divine assurance—this is all beyond the understanding of the man who has not yet given his heart into the Savior's keeping. As well talk to a blind man about the colors of the rainbow, or to a deaf man about the song of the nightingale, as try to explain the assurance of the Christian to a man who has not come to faith in Christ. This divine assurance is included in the revelation of which the Bible says, "What no eye has seen, nor ear heard, nor the heart of man imagined, what God has prepared for those who love Him."

Nor voice can sing, nor heart can frame,
Nor can the mem'ry find
A sweeter sound than Thy blest name,
O Savior of mankind!

O Hope of ev'ry contrite heart,
O Joy of all the meek!
To those who fall, how kind Thou art,
How good to those who seek!

But what to those who find? Ah! this
Nor tongue nor pen can show;
The love of Jesus, what it is,
None but His loved ones know.

A well-known life insurance company carries a picture of the Rock of Gibraltar on all of its advertising. The rock is the symbol of dependability. It suggests *assurance*. Wind and wave may wreak their havoc, time and tide may come and go, but the rock endures. Christ is the Christian's Rock. Millions have fled to that Rock for refuge and assurance in the familiar words of Toplady's immortal hymn:

> *Rock of Ages, cleft for me,*
> *Let me hide myself in Thee.*

Perhaps few people know better what it means to stand within the shelter of a rock than those who defended the island of Malta against the incessant German air bombardments in 1941. From the safe ledges of their rock-built caverns, they watched day after day— *unharmed*—as chaos and confusion swirled about them. Outside the rock, sure death would have been theirs. Inside the rock, no danger could befall them.

The rock to which the Christian flees when all the world seems to be caving in around him is the shelter of God's assurance, the assurance that God has given him in Christ. "Fear not, for

I am with you; be not dismayed, for I am your God; I will strengthen you, I will help you, I will uphold you with my righteous right hand."— "Fear not, for I have redeemed you; I have called you by name, you are Mine."

These and a thousand other assurances of God were clothed in a human personality when "the Word became flesh and dwelt among us." Jesus Christ is the personification of all God's assurances. He is the Rock of assurance, the Rock of salvation, in whom all mankind can find safety and security. Whatever God has offered to men in the way of spiritual assurance, He has offered to them through Christ. "I am the door," says Jesus, "If anyone enters by Me, he will be saved and will go in and out and find pasture."

I have found that pasture. Day after day my heart can feed on the assurances that Christ Himself has given me. He has assured me of His love, His care, His presence, His protection. These are the assurances on which I walk. These are the assurances by which I live. These are

the assurances that someday will give strength
to my wavering feet when I am called upon
to make that final, fateful journey through the
valley of death.

> *Blessed assurance, Jesus is mine!*
> *Oh, what a foretaste of glory divine!*
> *Heir of salvation, purchase of God,*
> *Born of His Spirit, washed in His blood!*

Joy

A British naval officer tells the story of a wealthy native of India who paid a tremendous price to become a Christian. "No sooner had he been baptized," writes the officer, "than all of his possessions were taken from him, and his wife and children disowned him." One day the officer asked the former rich man: "Are you able to bear your troubles?" The poor man replied: "Many people ask me that, but they never ask me whether I am able to bear my _joys_; for I enjoy a happiness in my heart since I know Christ which no one has been able to take from me."

The spiritual experience of this man has been the experience of every man, woman, and child who has ever put his faith in Jesus Christ as his personal Savior. I, too, have had the same experience. Of all the joys of life, I have found none greater, none more exciting, than the sure knowledge that, through Christ, God has become my Father, my sins have been washed away, and heaven is my assured possession.

The religion of Jesus Christ is essentially a religion of joy. It is a caricature of the truth to picture the Christian as a man with a long face, a heavy book, and a black umbrella. The life of Christ itself is a living contradiction of the claim that to be a consistent Christian one must be an apostle of gloom. The Savior mingled freely with the common people of His day, took part in their innocent pleasures, and hallowed their homely joys with the benediction of His presence. The Pharisees of His day frequently complained that Jesus was not as strict as John the Baptist, that He mingled too freely with common folks, and that His whole demeanor was lacking in the austerity and severity that they associated with a prophet. "This man receives sinners and eats with them," they murmured.

Christ had come to earth to proclaim a

religion of joy. Already on the night of His birth the angel messenger had announced: "Fear not, for behold, I bring you good news of great joy that will be for all the people. For unto you is born this day in the city of David, a Savior, who is Christ the Lord." Wherever He went, throughout His earthly life, He brought joy to the sorrowing, cheer to the downcast, and gladness to those who were sitting in the shadow of death. The supreme aim of His earthly ministry was to restore joy to human hearts that had been languishing in the shackles of sin and sadness.

It is significant how frequently the Savior referred to this joy on the night before His crucifixion. After speaking to His disciples at length concerning their intimate relationship with Him, which would continue even after His death and resurrection—using the familiar symbol of the vine and the branches—He says to them, "These things I have spoken to you, that My joy may be in you, and that your joy may be full." His continued presence in their lives was

to be a continuing source of joy and gladness—
also after they could no longer see Him. But as
the Savior peered into the future that night, He
could see the inevitable trials that would beset
the lives of those who put their trust in Him,
and so He assures His believers, "You will be
sorrowful, but your sorrow will turn into joy.
. . . And no one will take your joy from you."
Your joy will be your permanent possession.

Anyone who takes the time to read the
history of the Early Christian Church as it is
given in the books of the New Testament will
agree that *joy* was the dominant note of the
lives of Christ's apostles. This does not mean
that the lives of Christ's followers were cush-
ioned by beds of roses. No, there were hardships
to be endured. But they found joy in the midst
of hardship, gladness in the midst of pain. "As
sorrowful, yet always rejoicing; as poor, yet
making many rich" is the way the Bible puts it.

Thus, for instance, after Peter and his
companions had been beaten and thrown into
prison for having preached the Gospel, we

read that "they left the presence of the council, rejoicing that they were counted worthy to suffer dishonor for the name." And later on we are told that after Paul and Silas had been cruelly beaten and thrown into the inner dungeon, "about midnight Paul and Silas were praying and singing hymns to God." They had experienced a joy that was so deep, so firm, so sure that the trials of life were but as the ripples on the surface of the sea. Their joy was undisturbed. "No one will take your joy from you."

And they were eager that others become partakers of their joy. Again and again we hear them offering the joy of the Gospel, the joy of salvation, to others. "Rejoice in the Lord always; again I will say, Rejoice," St. Paul writes to his Philippians. "Rejoice always," is his exhortation to the Thessalonians. Enumerating the blessings of the Christian faith, Paul writes to the Galatians: "But the fruit of the Spirit is love, joy, peace," and to the Romans he writes, "For the kingdom of God is . . . righteousness and peace and joy in the Holy Spirit." And

Peter writes to the Christians who had been scattered throughout Asia Minor that, since they have come to a knowledge of salvation through faith in the blood of their Redeemer, they now "rejoice with joy that is inexpressible and filled with glory." To Christ, to His apostles, and to the early Christians, the message of the Gospel was a message of joy—and the life of the believer was a life of gladness based upon that message.

> *Oh, for a thousand tongues to sing*
>   *My great Redeemer's praise,*
> *The glories of my God and King,*
>   *The triumphs of His grace!*
>
> *Jesus! The name that charms our fears,*
>   *That bids our sorrows cease;*
> *'Tis music in the sinner's ears,*
>   *'Tis life and health and peace.*

The joy of the Christian, says the Bible, is a joy "in the Lord." It finds its reason in Christ. The permanence of our joy usually depends upon the reason for our joy. The joy of the child who has just been given an ice cream cone will be short-lived because of the passing nature of the object of its joy. The joy of the young man who finds supreme satisfaction in the exercise of his youthful vigor will begin to fade as youth gives way to old age. The joy of the young lady who has found her highest good in her charm and beauty will last no longer than these attractions. And the joy of the businessman who has attached his heart to wealth and influence will crumble into dust on the day that his possessions are taken from him. Yes, it is true, the permanence of our joy depends upon the reason for our joy. That is why the Christian's joy is always "in the Lord."

Some time ago I came across these remarkable paragraphs. In answer to the question *Where Is Happiness?* the anonymous author answers:

Not in Unbelief—

Voltaire was an infidel of the most pronounced type. He wrote, "I wish I had never been born."

Not in Pleasure—

Lord Byron lived a life of pleasure, if anyone did. He wrote, "The worm, the canker, and the grief are mine alone."

Not in Money—

Jay Gould, the American millionaire, had plenty of that. When dying, he said, "I suppose I am the most miserable man on earth."

Not in Position and Fame—

Lord Beaconsfield enjoyed more than his share of both. He wrote, "Youth is a mistake; manhood, a struggle; old age, a regret."

Not in Military Glory—

Alexander the Great conquered the known world in his day. Having done so, he wept in his tent, because, he said, "There are no more worlds to conquer."

Where, Then, Is Happiness Found?

The answer is simple: In Christ alone. He said, "I will see you again, and your hearts

will rejoice, and no one will take your joy
from you."

What Jesus was to His disciples and to
the believers of the Early Church, He is still
to millions of believing souls throughout the
world today. The Christian is the happiest man
in all the world. In fact, no one in all the world
has a better right to joy and gladness than the
trusting child of God. He alone knows beyond
the shadow of a doubt that all his sins have
been forgiven and that through Christ he has
a clear title to a mansion in the Father's house
above. He alone has the divine assurance of
comfort in sorrow, strength in sickness, solace
in bereavement, help in distress, and ultimate
triumph in the midst of dire calamity. And this
assurance is signed and sealed in the blood of
the Son of God Himself. The world has known
no higher guarantee.

This joy, the unspeakable joy of the child
of God, is mine. I have found that no matter
what the circumstance, no matter how fraught

with gloom the prospect, no matter how discouraging or disconcerting the difficulty, I could nevertheless tap that reservoir of joy that God has placed into every human heart that has come to Him through Christ. The assurance of His pardon, His peace, His power, His presence in every scene of life, has emptied my life of gloom and sadness and filled it with a high and holy gladness. It was this deep and all-pervading assurance that moved the learned Horatius Bonar to exclaim:

> *All that I was, my sin, my guilt,*
> *My death, was all mine own;*
> *All that I am I owe to Thee,*
> *My gracious God, alone.*

> *The evil of my former state*
> *Was mine, and only mine;*
> *The good in which I now rejoice*
> *Is Thine, and only Thine.*

> *The darkness of my former state,*
> *The bondage, all was mine;*

The light of life in which I walk,
　　The liberty, is Thine.

Thy Word first made me feel my sin,
　　It taught me to believe;
Then, in believing, peace I found,
　　And now I live, I live!

What does Jesus mean to me? He means joy, joy unspeakable, joy already here on earth and eternally in heaven!

Heaven

A little girl was walking with her father along a country road. The night was clear, and the child was enthralled by the splendor of the sky, all lit up with twinkling stars from one end to the other. After moments of reflection, she suddenly looked up to her father and said: "Daddy, I was just thinking—if the *wrong* side of heaven is so beautiful, how wonderful the *right* side must be!"

No tongue or pen has ever succeeded in describing the glory, the grandeur, and the magnificence of the Father's house above. That it is a place of entrancing beauty and matchless splendor, the apostle John indicates in the Book of Revelation by describing heaven's glories in terms of costly jewels and precious gems and rarest metals.

How could heaven be anything else but beautiful! It is the habitation of our God, the royal palace of the King of kings! And in that palace—oh, wondrous thought—the Son of God has gone to prepare a place for those who trust Him as their Savior. Through faith in His redeeming mercy, they will ascend someday to His home beyond the skies—more exquisite, more glorious, more wonderful than human speech can tell!

> *Jerusalem the golden,*
> *With milk and honey blest—*
> *The promise of salvation,*
> *The place of peace and rest—*
> *We know not, oh, we know not*
> *What joys await us there:*
> *The radiancy of glory,*
> *The bliss beyond compare!*

Yes, I know not what joys await me there: but I do know, as sure as God's own Word is true, that heaven's glories shall be mine. And I have found this immovable assurance in Jesus Christ, my Savior. One of the most tender chapters in the entire Bible is that passage that describes the solemn meeting of the Savior with His faithful few on the night in which He was betrayed. There, in the very shadow of approaching death, Jesus comforted His despondent followers with the memorable words: "Let not your hearts be troubled. . . . In My Father's house are many rooms. If it were not so, would I have told you that I go to prepare a place for you? And if I go and prepare a place for you, I will come again and will take you to Myself, that where I am you may be also." Those words of Jesus Christ, my Savior, mean more to me than all the gold and silver of a thousand hills!

There is something about the life beyond the grave that fills our hearts with dreadful awe and solemn wonder. Even the thought of heaven—with its unspeakable glory and grandeur—sometimes frightens us, and we ask: "Will I feel at home in heaven? Will I be at ease

in the celestial mansions?" How wonderfully all
our fears, all our misgivings are silenced when,
with the Savior, we can point to heaven and say:
"My Father's house!" Through Christ, the Ruler
of the rolling spheres has become my Father,
and going to heaven is a happy homecoming, a
blessed reunion of the Father with His children.
What comfort, what strength, what joy are
mine—in the knowledge that beyond the
portals of eternity there lies a friendly Father's
house!

As the Savior that night looked out across the
centuries and saw all the countless throngs who
would be brought to faith in Him, He thought
it fitting to remind them that the expanse of His
Father's house is limitless—there will be room
enough for all who come to the Father through
faith in Him. And so He assures His followers,
"In My Father's house are many rooms."

I may be sure: there is room enough for me!
He whose love singled me out as an object of
His all-redeeming mercy and who has promised
to preserve me unto the day of His heavenly

kingdom—He has prepared and reserved a room for me. He has claimed and is holding my place in the eternal mansions. "I know whom I have believed, and I am convinced that He is able to guard until that Day," says the apostle Paul. "Henceforth there is laid up for me the crown of righteousness, which the Lord, the righteous judge, will award to me on that Day, and not only to me but also to all who have loved His appearing."

There is something significant about every reference of the Savior to His Father's house. He speaks as one who has been there! "If it were not so, would I have told you?" As one who stands on a mountaintop looking down into the valley beyond and telling his comrades behind him what he sees, so the Savior tells us about His Father's house and ours. The streets of the eternal city are familiar to Him. The rooms of the Father's house stand clear and bright before His vision. He *knows* what lies beyond the valley, because He has come from there. That is why He could speak of heaven and say: "If it were not so, would I have told you?" What a strengthening assurance to have as one's dearest friend Him who has already spent endless ages in the eternal Father's house, who knows the way, and who by His innocent suffering and death for our sins upon the cross has opened up that way for us! Into the hands of such a divine Redeemer we can surely entrust our souls for time and for eternity.

There was another tender note of reassurance in the words that Christ spoke to His faithful few that night, a note that has poured faith and courage into the hearts of Christian people ever since. "I will come again." As a mother soothes her weeping child from whom she must be parted for a moment with the whisper of assurance, "I will come again," so the Savior seeks to soothe the fears of His disciples with the comforting assurance of His imminent return. I must leave you now, He says, but—"Let not your hearts be troubled. . . . I will come again."

And how effectively that simple promise of the Savior instilled fresh courage into their fainting hearts throughout the coming years is seen from Bible history. Trials and afflictions, pains and persecutions—all would have to be borne, to be sure—but only until He would come again. Then all would be supremely well. His coming, either at the death of the world or at the death of His disciples, cast a golden glow over all the road that lay ahead. They were walking toward the light of His return. And in that light all shadows fell behind them.

So, too, in the lives of all who have put their trust in the might and mercy of the Savior. All sorrows, all heartaches, all disappointments and bereavements lose their bitterness in the sweetness of the Savior's tender promise: "I will come again." I will come again to turn your sorrows into joy, your heartaches into gladness, your bereavements into heavenly reunions in My Father's house above.

It was that same night that Jesus prayed to His Father and said: "Father, I desire that they also, whom you have given Me, may be with Me where I am, to see My glory that you have given Me because you loved Me before the foundation of the world." He shares with His Father a desire that, when He repeats it to His disciples, becomes a promise: "I will come again and will take you to Myself, that where I am you may be also." Jesus has secured His Father's approval and permission to bring His friends with Him to share His glory in the Father's house. By His suffering, death, and resurrection, He has unlocked the door of His Father's home—and heaven has become an open house! That is why He could say, "Where I am you may be also"—you who have come to the Father by Me "may be also."

> *"Forever with the Lord!"*
>   *Amen! so let it be.*
>   *Life from the dead is in that word,*
>   *'Tis immortality.*

But can I be sure that Christ has the power to fulfill these promises? Yes, I can be sure!

Why? Because Christ Himself has risen from the dead and proved Himself the victor over sin and death and hell. More than sixty years after His death and resurrection and ascension into heaven, He appeared to His beloved apostle John (the man who recorded the comforting words of the Savior about the rooms of His Father's house) and said to him, "I am . . . the living one. I died, and behold I am alive forevermore, and I have the keys of Death and Hades." By His resurrection from the dead, Christ proved Himself the Son of God with power to keep His promises. His victory over the grave is our pledge of life eternal. His empty tomb proclaims to us that someday our grave, too, shall be empty. "Because I live, you also will live," He assures every one of His believers. "I am the resurrection and the life. Whoever believes in Me, though he die, yet shall he live, and everyone who lives and believes in Me shall never die." It was because of Christ's resurrection that the apostle could exclaim: "O death, where is your victory? O death, where is your sting? The sting of death is sin, and the power of sin is the law. But thanks be to God, who gives us the victory through our Lord Jesus Christ." And the same apostle says in another passage: "But in fact Christ has been raised from the dead, the firstfruits of those who have fallen asleep." Just as the firstfruits are the foretaste of the later and more general harvest, so Christ's resurrection is the guarantee of our resurrection to life immortal—in that later, greater harvest. Christ's resurrection is God's final stamp of approval on the redeeming work of His Son. And now—because He lives, we, too, shall live.

> *I know that my Redeemer lives;*
> *What comfort this sweet sentence gives!*
> *He lives, He lives, who once was dead;*
> *He lives, my everliving head.*
>
> *He lives to bless me with His love;*
> *He lives to plead for me above;*
> *He lives my hungry soul to feed;*
> *He lives to help in time of need.*

He lives and grants me daily breath;
He lives, and I shall conquer death;
He lives my mansion to prepare;
He lives to bring me safely there.

Yes, "He lives to bring me safely there." In that distant home lies the complete fulfillment of all my highest hopes. There dwells my Savior, who has prepared my mansion for me—and has prepared me for my mansion. There dwell those whom "I love most and best." And there—blessed thought!—I, too, someday shall dwell!

And I shall dwell there solely because of the unmerited goodness and grace of God, whose gift to all believers "is eternal life in Christ Jesus our Lord." Small wonder that the greatest apostle of them all, as he contemplated the vexations and the vanities of this present world, could say during the closing years of his life: "My desire is to depart and be with Christ, for that is far better." And again: "For to me to live is Christ, and to die is gain."

What does Jesus mean to me?

Chief of sinners though I be,
Jesus shed His blood for me,
Died that I might live on high,
Lives that I might never die.
As the branch is to the vine,
I am His, and He is mine.

Index to Bible Passages

A list of all Bible passages quoted in this book, arranged according to the sequence in which they appear on each page.

Page 11
Psalm 51:5
Genesis 8:21
Ephesians 2:3

Page 12
Psalm 49:7–8
Acts 4:12
Galatians 4:4–5

Page 13
Philippians 3:9

Page 14
Isaiah 53:4–6
Matthew 20:28
1 Corinthians 11:24
Matthew 26:28

Page 15
John 3:14–16
1 Corinthians 15:3
Romans 5:10
1 John 1:7
1 Peter 2:24
Galatians 2:20
Galatians 3:13
1 Peter 1:18–19

Page 16
1 John 2:1–2
Romans 8:1
Romans 8:31–39

Page 22
John 14:27
John 16:33

Page 23
1 John 2:15–16

Page 24
Ephesians 2:14
Romans 7:24
Ephesians 2:14

Page 25
Romans 5:1
Romans 15:13
Philippians 4:7

Page 28
Luke 2:29–30
Psalm 23:4

Page 29
Isaiah 26:3
Deuteronomy 33:27
Lamentations 3:23
Colossians 3:3

Page 34
John 15:4–5

Page 35
Philippians 4:13
Galatians 2:20
Philippians 4:13
Galatians 2:20

Page 37
2 Corinthians 3:5
1 Corinthians 15:10
Romans 1:4
Hebrews 1:3
Matthew 28:18

Index to Hymns

The following hymns from *Lutheran Service Book* (*LSB*)
and *The Lutheran Hymnal* (*TLH*) are quoted in this book.

Herman W. Gockel was involved in an effective writing ministry from the time of his graduation from Concordia Seminary, St. Louis, in 1931. While a parish pastor, he made a significant contribution to religious journalism by writing newspaper sermonettes for weekly publication. For two years, he headed the "spiritual problem" department of the International Lutheran Hour, gaining deep insight for his later work. From 1952 until his retirement in 1971, Dr. Gockel served as religious director for the television program *This Is the Life*.

Dr. Gockel is probably best remembered for his work as coauthor of *A Child's Garden of Prayer* and numerous other devotional writings including *Daily Walk with God*.

In May of 1996, the Lord called Dr. Herman W. Gockel to his heavenly rest with the Church Triumphant. He will be remembered for many years to come through his distinctive writing style.